Y0-BYA-379

Pearl is a poetic exploration of the life of the legendary Pearl Miller, early Calgary's most famous and successful madam. Cullen fuses traditional lyric lines and experimental uses of form and language to fabricate an unexpected biography of Calgary's mythical brothel keeper.

Also by Nancy Jo Cullen:

Science Fiction Saint

Pearl

Nancy Jo Cullen

Frontenac House
Calgary, Alberta

Copyright © 2006 by Nancy Jo Cullen

All rights reserved, including moral rights. No part of this publication may be reproduced or transmitted in any form or by any means electronic or mechanical including photocopying, recording, or any information storage retrieval system without permission in writing from the author or publisher, or ACCESS copyright, except by a reviewer or academic who may quote brief passages in a review or critical study.

Book and cover design: Epix Design
Photo on cover and title page: Mugshot of Pearl Miller, Calgary Police Service Museum Society, used by permission of the Executive Director, Janet Pieschel.
Author photo: Deborah Cullen

Library and Archives Canada Cataloguing in Publication

Cullen, Nancy Jo
Pearl / Nancy Jo Cullen.

Poems.
ISBN 1-897181-03-5

I. Title.

PS8555.U473P43 2006   C811'.54   C2005-907654-2

We acknowledge the support of the Canada Council for the Arts which last year invested $20.3 million in writing and publishing throughout Canada. We also acknowledge the support of The Alberta Foundation for the Arts.

 Canada Council   Conseil des Arts
for the Arts   du Canada

Printed and bound in Canada
Published by Frontenac House Ltd.
1138 Frontenac Avenue S.W.
Calgary, Alberta, T2T 1B6, Canada
Tel: 403-245-2491   Fax: 403-245-2380
editor@frontenachouse.com   www.frontenachouse.com

1 2 3 4 5 6 7 8 9   11 10 09 08 07 06

UNIVERSITY LIBRARY
UNIVERSITY OF ALBERTA

For my mom, Mary Florence Hickey, who shared with me her love of stories.

Acknowledgements

I owe sincere thanks to the following folks: The Alberta Foundation for the Arts for their financial support of this project in its early stages; Suzette Mayr for keeping me sharp and on track; Tere Mahoney and Rachael Joo at the Calgary Police Archives, who went well beyond their call of duty in getting the image of Pearl Miller for me, as well as Jennifer Palmer who found the listings of Pearl Miller's early arrests (and saved me hours and hours of searching) and Janet Pieschel who gave us permission to use the images; the Rev. Dr. John Pentland for taking the time to talk with me about salvation by sharing his perspective, engaging with mine and never once trying to convert me; my family for taking such good care of me through a very difficult year and Debbie and Bruce for the inspirational trip. Finally, I am deeply indebted to John Lefebvre whose breathtaking support has made everything possible, I hope I do you proud. The accident of birth has been very good to me.

Contents

Preamble

Pearl Miller was a legendary madam from the early days of Calgary who catered to the community's elite. Over the course of 28 years she worked in and owned several bordellos. She even had the cheek to operate a bawdy house in lower Mount Royal, which, not surprisingly, aroused the authorities. In 1942, following countless hours of surveillance by the police and a total of three arrests, she was tried, convicted, and sentenced to three months in Fort Saskatchewan jail.

The whore known for her good manners and tasteful decorating style returned from Fort Saskatchewan a changed woman. At the age of sixty Mrs. Miller converted to Pentecostal Christianity and spent the remaining fifteen years of her life trying to save girls from the street. Jock Ritchie, one of the constables involved in her 1942 arrest, stated: "If I met her on the street she would speak in passing and, as I say, never seemed to bear any ill-will against us."

Imagine the buzz in Calgary's parlours in 1929 when a rich client identified only as "the son of one of Calgary's most prominent lawyers" set Pearl up in a big house south of the city at what is now Heritage and Macleod Drives. But aside from a few early arrests, the purchases of her houses and her later transformative imprisonment, the details of Pearl Miller's life remain sketchy. Pearl Rose (Miller's legal surname earned after a brief marriage that ended in divorce) arrived in Calgary in 1914 and died here in 1957. I don't suppose it's a surprise that the details of a whore's life have been lost to history but I find her story emblematic of the renegade individualism Alberta claims to love. This is a work of imagination based on that fading legend.

Fragment on History

the sheer and simple necessity of women's work
enobled by no myth
and the scarcity of summer
virgins and whores all omitted from

2 Seconds Before the Angels Hurt Her Feelings

Speaking to the Lord
And the angels
Heart unbuttoned and down around her ankles
Before fingers
Before
For that moment
Enduring on the wings of heaven
She believed
She was born to sing

She was a son of God in the brotherhood of fellowship when
man was all of them. 10 years old, aching for a little kindness
and she had one minute of the Holy Spirit with no one watching
especially herself.

She'd been wrestling with words to find angels in the desert. One
pure moment with her head attached to her shoulders her ankles
to her feet, one pure moment with everything calling her by her
name.

There is a particular clarity to innocence, for instance, the belief
in the benevolence of God & that the nature of man *is* nature.
This is an historical construction for which she is out of context.
Like Theresa, with her perfectly turned ankles (worth a small
fortune) who, after the death of her husband, showed a gift for
slaughtering chickens. But disclosure of immanence beckons,
supposedly immaterial.

And she had never been afraid of hard work.

Rossland, BC: Spring 1914

Eventually she will refer to him as *a man named Rose*

But this morning he is named John
He pulls at her arm, drags her back under the comforter
Her head bangs against the pillow
His weight delivers her of breath
Later, it will become evident he was taking his leave of her

She lights a fire
Next a cinematic kiss nearly John Wayne & Maureen O'Hara in
The Quiet Man (neither heroine exactly a girl) then his farewell
She begins to sweep, her intense dislike of the work subsumed by
a lifetime of sticking to the task at hand, of all that could be done
she thinks, *A batch of good light bread never comes amiss*

Sooner than not
the waiting begins, the silence of the day envelops the distance
between who she is and what she wants echoes
in such small rooms
She has become a wife in the chapel where English is spoken
Mrs. Rose clicks her tongue and sits (just briefly)
at the table near the window
It is a beautiful day, the air crisp, cold and inviting

And so she pulls
her coat around her shoulders, stands on the back stoop
breathes in the pine, mud, horse-shit, garbage and melting snow

Steps into the alley, follows the hill down
set to walk, before Tuesday becomes bread day, Wednesday
laundry day
She still believes the best is yet to come
It is well past a day before she learns the waiting is not that
he has not come home

Hearsay

Susceptible. She sits at her window. The mountains are looming. This winter the clouds have come to stifle her best-laid plans. She glances at her reflection; presumably this is what a stupid girl looks like although she is long past girl by anybody's standards.

Predisposed. She is sick of this weather. Outside of her window she hears children calling. "Pretend you are the big sister and pretend our parents are lost." "No. Pretend you are the baby and we are hiding from a nasty man." Their speculations are endless. She has heard enough.

Acquiescent. She has endured her father, his everlasting debits and credits; she has endured her brother, fawning over father. They would make the most of her failure; deliver her to the fate of a willful girl and hide her in their kitchen.

Scandalous. She lights a cigarette (her father would slap her if he were witness), rolls her head; despair and resistance crack along her shoulders. The surge of nicotine still causes her head to swim and she relishes the dizzy rush. "Pretend" she thinks, "Pretend nobody knows me yet."

Reluctant. A woman hurries her child down the steep road. They seem to be late, possibly lost. The woman is not familiar, nor the child, though it will not be long until they have heard of her. Her misfortune will be whispered into the ears of all well-bred women. She is their cautionary tale. The priest's proof of what happens to those who would defy the boundaries of denomination.

This is neither the beginning nor the end.

Becoming Salt

Hard seat pressing against her back
she tugs the band from her left finger
leans her head against the cool pane of glass
considers the perfect *oh* of gold resting in her palm
and tightens her fist around its surprise

Anger and grief rise in her throat and are swallowed
like the weather unable to rise above
the crowded pines and mountains
(after the fierce cold sun of the prairie she will remember with
nostalgia the grey that dominated these winters)
She is leaving the mountain for the plain
turning to the city and looking not behind

The gold band asserts itself, better now a wife than a maiden
She places the ring on her left finger
lifts her head and looks forward
only forward

Parental Consent Is Advised

Premised on the expansion of capitalist commodity production
Harlots rode the trains out west
Alberta the fair, the rich, the progressive
Leaping forth in the newness of life
Members of one body (wink, nudge)
The potential for both harm and good in the coming changes

The character of ideology in culture is to naturalize the norm
Consumer goods subject to standardization:
Whores, cars, clocks, etc
Position ever important in living relations
Missionary, skirts around your hips, etc
Pseudo-individualization
Each lady adhering to a strict formula
Aware of how every meeting will end

The coming potential for expressions and attractions
Preserve the status quo
Nellie vs Lulu
The sporting fashions of 1914
The normal school choir
Dry as the valley described by the prophet Ezekiel
A porcelain doll carried across the continent
The foundation of your belief
And, of course, of mine

The Name Game

Virgins	Whores
Mary	Mary
Nellie	Lucille
Irene	Lottie
Bella	May
Elizabeth	Addie
Jane	Dolly
Julia	Irene
Martha	Louise
Florence	Audrey
Ruth	Hannah
Muriel	Sadie
Henrietta	Charity
Emily	Millie
Faith	Flo
Cora	Rose
Anne	Alice
Margaret	Ruby
Agnes	Lily
Dorothea	Josephine
Catherine	Carmen
Clara	Mabel
Victoria	Lulu
Helen	Billie
Myrtle	Daisy

Pearl Pearl bo bearl
Banana fana fo fearl
Me mi mo mearl
Pearl!

Best Home Town I Know

I have been described as: squat and homely given to outlandish
rouge and makeup; the most famous woman in the history of
Cowtown (the horse-smellingest city in the west); a keeper of a
common bawdy-house; vagrant; itinerant
All this from a town that claims to love enterprise

Calgary rose and invited the sons of the empire to join her and
they brought their good wives and daughters struck dumb by the
tasks that loomed before them
Indeed we were ladies of leisure
Surely if it is a crime to use one's body for economic gain outside the
bounds of marriage then women shall become criminal

Our mothers named us for a different life: Charity, Hannah,
May, Sweet Alice
Our mothers named us for laundry and babies, sod walls and
endless winters
Perhaps it was the open land, sleep deprivation, love, etc
We became a world of our own
Japanése, Negro, and white women lived together
Evidence of the social consequences of unchastity

Ladies should have thanked us for the trouble we kept away
We had no theory, no text, no bio
But we aged as all good daughters did
Only our hands looked softer

Why

Because you are hungry
And because everybody loves a good time and definitely because
you were drunk and you were drunk because whatever brought
you to this God-forsaken, wind blown, rank cow town bursting
at the seams with possibility and no real work for a woman
except maybe unpaid schoolteacher which (just shoot you now)
you are the furthest thing from though you never really thought
of hussy as your first career choice. Seamstress maybe, but what
with all the soldiers floating around this town and liquor stopped
not by choice of the boys off to defend our so-called freedom and
being just tired of hoping that the grocer will trust your honest
eyes and tomorrow you will find some work that pays enough to
keep you and because of the looming threat of a drastic drop in
temperature and because your mother was consumptive and your
father, who was a decent working man, wrongly thought a farm
in the south of Alberta would be your salvation when, in fact, it
was the opposite and it drove him to the brink of hopelessness
and left him there to fester and your brothers found work as
ranch hands with nothing left to help a girl in a town without
a single garment factory but a whole lot of men willing to pay
more than that and a lot fewer hours too, I might add, with
maybe enough to take yourself to some more temperate place
someday where a husband might come along who thinks you a
widow or some other reason for knowing the things you happen
to have learned in the course of putting food in your belly and a
roof over your head.

Because you were pretty
Not that it mattered in the nature of this work and certainly not because you were led astray any time before the epiphany of the inescapable trouble you found yourself in and you didn't fancy yourself a wife to a poorly educated lout, or some fellow who didn't speak a lick of English and the others were all married off but not so nice as they didn't want to pay you for a little toss in a small back room of a pleasant looking house on the east side of the city and not because you loved it or because you hated it or anybody was looking to harm you in any real way but because it happened to be a man's world and a good reputation seemed less valuable than surviving and the other girls were nice and pretty much in the same boat as you, somewhat surprised to be here but also capable enough to take care of themselves whatever bloody place they came from, one as far as Japan and she could work 24 hours solid if she so chose, men finding her soft English and sharp hair so different from their European wives and sisters that even if it was only once they didn't want to go to the grave not knowing that in the end and for the amount of time spent on the matter it's all pretty much the same because this business is all about turnover no matter what anybody would like to think and finally, after cleaning the homes of those fine ladies you found it preferable to give head to their husbands.

Because they are small
Because time is imperfect
Because of a drastic drop in temperature
Because of fragrant lilacs

Because of the length of a summer night
Because of your mother
Because you forgot your father
Because you hate your feet

Because of dirty sticky floors
Because you squander time
Because you think you should
Because they want you to

Because you pluck your eyebrows
Because you should have a garden
Because you were drunk
Because you were a teenaged girl

Because you love to fuck
Because this time you won't
Because you were pretty
Because you can't say no

Because you want to make it better
Because you haven't heard of band aids
Because you can't read maps
Because you turned your back on God

Because you want to go to heaven
Because it's time for bed
Because you are hungry
Because everybody loves a good time

Because it's raining it's pouring
Because I said so
Because your stomach looks fat
Because even the most abstruse works of philosophical criticism
Need heed

To Whom It May Concern:

With
A dynamite first sentence you can grab the reader's attention
Aim for a friendly, yet respectful style that initiates rapport:

My Darling Darling,
Please knock before entering and
Don't fence me in my dear
Darling

Dear Sir or Madam,
What do you do with a drunken sailor
What do you do with a drunken sailor
What do you do with a drunken sailor
Er'lie in the morning

Take a letter Maria,
Address it to my life

Dearest Papa,
How are you?
Although the weather here is changeable I am fine, still
I worry
Can you shorten the distance between theory and practice?

Warmest regards,

Purveyor of Pussy

In those days we females were all more or less in the same line of work. It's just that my terms were cash.

Now what most appealed to me about my profession was that it was task oriented. Not the endless drudgery of housework. Not especially pleasant, but bearable. Not the sort of job I'd suppose you'd take to, sitting there at your desk. I suspect that you enjoy the nature of ink, how it spills across the page, stains the bottom of your thumb. And when you are angry how it sprays from your fingers like a shout. But me, I was born a working girl.

No, ladies didn't much care for a whore like me.

By the End of the Great War

We heard that some 40,000 men and boys had passed through
our camp
Off to face all the splendor of murder and mustard gas

There was a great fortune to be made as the glamour of the
war paled. We set our tents up just north of that glorified block
of shops folks referred to as Sarcee City. Those soldiers were
anxious to feel the world between their legs before they shipped
off to slaughter, each boy knowing he was as likely as the next
to be gone for all eternity. And not many were prepared to
meet their fate without at least one dip into the honey pot since
Sunday morning relieved them of all promise of hell, except the
earthly one they were sailing toward.

One boy in particular stands out in my memory
Hearty and pink with a fondness for sweets
He had no appetite for alcohol
A boyish adoration for his king and
A whore who was twice his age

I let him kiss me goodbye

Relief

The roaring twenties shuddered to a halt on the heels of the
Spanish Flu. The wind blowing farms to dust and boys and
soldiers back to the city.

Calgary grew up fast through drought, grasshopper plague,
wheat rust & sawfly. A city without a drink to offer the law-
abiding brokenhearted.

Being fed one square meal a day, divided into three portions,
the talk among the indigent turned to revolution.

The trade of token services for relief encouraged entertainment.
The most ambitious sort including a good fuck and some
whiskey.

Hard times we laughed in the small bedrooms allotted to our
services.

Hard, hard times.

1919 Prohibition Days

These were the days when it was a shame to be skinny
How it indicated doubtful nerves, lack of sleep
Friendlessness

Charity had the eye of a doctor, with her shorn flapper hair and
a young boy's chest. The good doctor had been on a ship in the
Dardenelles during the war where he developed a number of
addictions not the least of which was a pleasure in young girls.
Charity was seventeen but could easily pass for younger and
found the doctor more than willing to write prescriptions of
whiskey for the prevention of chills and relief from being too
skinny.

Now whores are not always the most organized of folk but
Charity had a swift business keeping working girls and their ilk
in supply of whiskey. Of course her boyish thighs demanded a
great price as well. One Sunday morning not too long after I
had purchased my first Model T for a tidy sum (slowing down
my progress toward a house considerably) Charity said to me
"Mama," which spoke as loudly about our looks as our age
difference. "Take me to Banff, I need some fresh mountain air."
And she pulled a quart of fine scotch out from behind her back.

I have always believed in a healthy balance of work and play and
when that little girl with her Marcel waves and endless laughter
in the face of all indignity bounced on the edge of my tired bed I
decided the National Park System might do well by the visit of a
couple of whores.

Lord knows Canmore's miners did

It Was a Slim and Lethal Summer

And a skinny child has nothing left with which to fight
The unbearable heat contained within a weekend
Contained within a body
Feverish

We watched her pass from cough to tornado
All thunder and wind coursing through her skin
Struggling against water, against breath

This woman who made an industry of looking girl
Drowning
And us so helpless in the fury her body was riding

I beat my fists against her back
She whispered "Mamma that hurts like hell
Stop"

There are so many days about this girl I cannot recall

526 - 9 Avenue SE

Oh fairest house to shelter easy girls,
That thereby carnal lust shall never die,
And thy parlour shall host the tender churl,
Who leaving wife at home with whore doth lie.
Six hundred square feet and no mortgage due,
Although the city starves, thy walls shall flourish.
Harlots give proof of what man will pursue
Though work be lost and children be malnourished.
Fellas whilst your cocks point ever north,
Let my house be this town's best ornament,
Abound with postures towards good manners
And within my girls buriest thy content!
      I purchase this year, nineteen twenty-six,
      Investment in old age by pleasing dicks.

Mi Casa es Su Casa

What do I want? What should I say? What does she want? Are we a story or a secret? Patience, willpower and the things we keep. What do we tell? It might not have been a respectable house but it was decent. Whether there were feelings of power or of being tarnished it was a job to make it feel like a home; a home where your wife would talk dirty. We were all boarders in the fictional house.

Home for the Holidays

Christmas Eve, the streets immobilized by the
fierceness of winter,
Spousal expectation and children stretched with anticipation
All the world made WCTU perfect

It was our custom to celebrate the birth of our Lord with gin,
Goose cooked to perfection and euchre, May being the sort of
girl who had trouble counting the cards involved in bridge and
all of us wanting peace more than trump
Of all May's accomplishments card playing was the least but she
sang well enough to bring tears to our eyes
Ave Maria
She broke our hearts during the three minutes we pretended we
were something other than whores and eligible for an invitation
to the world prescribed by history

Boxing Day was back to business with a vengeance
All the wooden pews, Christmas oranges and shrill children
Coming to roost in my house
It was a regular Boxing Day Blowout

May came to me a choir girl
Never comprehending the importance of a right bower
Each year she spent Boxing Day quiet in the kitchen
Picking at her lips
Refusing to sing and waiting for
December 27

The Standard Language of (Pearl's) Girls:

Ciao Bella!

As a young woman I often felt I laughed too loudly, anything above a sweet twitter from a girl an indication of being disreputable. By the time I became a reputable widow I was worn down by the poverty of respectability. The Spanish influenza was fearsome indeed, left me with the feeling that I needed to find work that was recession proof.

Buon Natale!

Convention held that a woman who let herself be taken advantage of by a man in the hopes of getting a marriage proposal was utterly destitute of moral principal and virtue. That's just a whole bunch of words designed to remove the complications. His parents had other plans for him, and he was the eldest son. I arrived in Calgary in early December. So much for hope, and snow.

Parla inglese?

team slut

Lady's man, Tomcat, Master, Lord of the dance, Mr. Speaker, Your Honour, Captain, Private, High-muck-a-muck, Reverend, Father, Mr. Big, Sir.

fallen woman

Hell's Half Acre

Naphtha put us all on the map so to speak.
That spring gas poured forth in such abundance bringing about a
surge of hope (and other parts) in men.
Turner Valley glowed day and night and darkness became
gesture. The day remained held for swindlers and night
beckoned those looking for an end to the penury of farming this
unforgiving soil.

(I suppose the worst thing for hookers was the sexual revolution
of girls that occurred shortly after my day and which, I dare say,
removed the necessity, for many men, to pay for favours. What
the Lord was more likely to frown on is beyond me to guess
having spent so many years on the edge of respect. Whether for
economic gain or not, I counselled against such actions, knowing
men to be debased creatures, largely incapable of attachment,
leaving women forever hoping.)

Yes, when Royalite No. 4 spewed its promise of wealth against
the backdrop of the foothills and all that is cowboy movie about
this place I raised my face to the sky and gave thanks because if
I could have nothing else I could have wealth; living evidence,
even back then, that all was not well within the framework of
respectability. I enjoyed making that point.

That Strange Dream, 1929

1

When Pearl dreamed of Mr. _____ Esq. (as he liked to be
    called)
She dreamed of his penchant for making money
She dreamed of his heir sitting in a rumble seat and
She dreamed she was driving down Stephen Avenue laughing
Hannah was standing in front of the Bay; she waved
Pearl called "I'm the carriage driver" over and over
Hannah was repeating an indecipherable chant

2

In the dream she could think through her fingers and
The shape of her garden and
The taste of her supper and
When she stumbled on the clutter she thought:
A place for everything and everything in its place
It is not through chance
Don't bite off more than you can chew

3

Then she dreamed she took her secrets to her grave and
    everybody made up stories
Oh the ideas they come up with!
She heard voices (Hannah, was it Hannah who called?) repeating
    the following:
Do you insist on your capacity
To change your circumstances?
Are you jargon-ridden?
Anti-essentialist?
Are you looking for an intellectual counter?
Can you chop vegetables on it?

4
At 47 Pearl dreamed she saw the future and it had nothing to do
    with her
A mother who could recall precious little remembered the name
    of the famous whore
And Hannah, at the edge of the dream, kept calling
I'm here to testify that Jesus has cured me of the habit of
    masturbation.

Now why would Hannah do a fool thing like that?

5
When Pearl awoke she brewed a strong pot of coffee then she
called Mr. _____ Esq. at his daddy's office, there was a
fieldstone house just south of the city she'd been thinking of.

Concatenation

(all you've ever wanted)

First, a fear of profundity
and unqualified unhappiness

A peripatetic polemicist
eating butter tarts from The Palmetto Bakery

The North West Mounted Police prior to registered trademarks
(didn't call them Mounties for nothing)

Reformers more interested in preventing prostitution

Then, Salvation

A peripatetic polemicist wearing lipstick
looking for the levels of hierarchy

Overarching obsessions
defined by place
(as in everything in its)

Ignoring the economic, sexist and psychological factors involved

Sweet Alice Speaks

My father didn't want me going out with no boys. He figured
the first thing I was gonna do was bring him home some bastard
when my intentions were nothing of the sort.

So I come home one night and he's waiting for me
Last thing I felt was his hard fist in my face
He filled my mother's sitting room with blood
He had the hands of a stonemason
Turned my sweet little nose into a mushroom
Seems he saw some girl walking along the tracks and it sparked
an idea

In his head I needed to be taught a lesson
This is what I had to live with
And I did and I survived
And I never brought home no bastard

I brought my bastard here. Mrs. Miller was setting up her big
house. It seemed as good a job as any. In the end I thought it
fitting I should make my daddy's dreams come true.

My mother lived the rest of her days with that man.

Fun Was Where We Found It

And you'd be surprised what money can be made
In hard times
The winter of 1932 still found us with cash in the coffer
Though cattlemen didn't cross our porch
With the same frequency
Money begets money

Millie was always a cut-up at the piano
And with Lulu who spent six months working at my place
We had a regular Sunday night vaudeville act
Lulu was so full of MGM ideas

I wanted to tell her to take care
I've never met a man who wasn't shamed
By such a wife's career
Instead I gave her one hundred dollars
Watched her follow love, a white ribbon tied through her hair
And drive east into the unprecedented trials of
The Great Depression

You can't blame a girl for trying

Westward Ho

Because it requires a buyer and a seller, prostitution is most effectively defined as the practice of exchanging money for sexual services.

Prohibited prostitution-related activities:
- procuring or living on the avails of prostitution,
- owning, operating or occupying a bawdy house,
- all forms of public communication for the purpose of prostitution,
- knowingly transporting another to a bawdy house.

Well, I catered to men with ample financial means and all sorts of things were discussed in those small rooms. We celebrated the birth of children not our own, planned investments, commiserated about the weather. We built a dialogue of innuendo as well as friendships of sorts, and treated none of it as business. As the gracious hostess I received no public recognition, except in the form of hyperbole and myth. I would say a fair number of those men considered themselves gentlemen, at their first visit, told themselves they were unwitting dupes.

Of course their manners were, by and large, impeccable.

The Lord's Plan

Hannah went crazy then she turned to the Lord
He took her in as is
Left her on the corner of Stephen Avenue confessing her sins
Calling out to the hopeless

Initially we thought it was sleep deprivation
But she insisted on her madness
Pulled away from my house and took on Jesus
Lost her memory

With no anger to drive her on she crumbled
More delicate than her milkmaid hands foretold
Daily she testified to the innocent and rueful
Magnifying the satisfaction of good people

And I laughed with the rest
At the crazy girl bearing witness to all that Jesus might cure
I failed that girl

I failed that girl

The Future of Scent

Before the everyday use of plastic:
Mud, horse shit and burning coal
A damp wool blanket
Diesel, spat from the train
Fungal sheets, jism
Rye splashed against a windowsill
A brisk westerly delivering dust
and the promise of spring, or winter depending on which corner
you stood

The odor of a pipe, sweet until after the Spanish flu then
sorrowful
Vinegar on the morning floors
The ears of an unwashed man (always too close to the nose)
The piss of a tomcat on an inside wall
A new deck of cards
Rosewater and glycerin rubbed lightly on tired skin,
Funereal in retrospect

Cloves inside a tooth
Baked apples
The tight smell of ten days of thirty below zero
Fresh cut lilacs in a bowl (again, in retrospect, funereal)
Toast and saskatoon jelly

Regret unmitigated by capital assets

Working Girls

*It is now time to tell you that it is not through chance that the right
margins are even in all the timed writings. Each line had to be revised
many times, and it was quite a job. When you do other kinds of work,
you must realize that you will not have straight right margins.*
- Modern Typewriting Manual of Office Procedure

Always in the business of reversing fortune, you might say
making lemonade from lemons.
A simple understanding of understanding.
All of us looking to be a lily among the thorns.

Different from those girls, because that's what everybody called
them then, clacking away on their old smith coronas. Presumably
waiting for a husband, the odd one sharp as Katherine Hepburn.
(She might have even slapped a fella in the face. Sometime
shortly after, of course, her elocutionary star had faded.)
Those girls carried the stern grace of revision.
They had no room for error.

Oh daughters of Jerusalem!

What Remains in Mind:

How the law forgot its manners when no one was watching
Chivalry was abandoned and loud jokes replaced the overdone
sexuality men pretend to
That was the first of our punishments

All bowed down to profit, swindlers, whores and Christians
Of course only swindlers and Christians were invited to tea

Red sky at night, a sailor's delight
Red sky in morning, sailor take warning

Hannah always cried easily
The constant threat of arrest made me tired to the bone.

The wise know God's limits,
Fools know no bounds

Pithy

Prima Facie

The hounds of society were circling my door and just weeks after
my first conviction prompted by the Good Citizens who wanted
me (like their maids and Indians) to be trouble-free and ready
to perform upon request, the dogs came barking. I announced
our friends the police to my girls who made haste to dress while
I fumbled at the door. And as the girls pulled on their stockings
the eager sergeant took the stairs two at a time. I braced myself
against the newel and listened to the lonely tune in my head.

There I was, *one of the last of the old red light district madams*
watching half-dressed girls file downstairs followed by my
fine clients, abashed and ready to play upright husband. My
father had never cared for my success, never understood what
I had gleaned while sitting in the back of his life. I had made a
booming business consorting with the men he, the sycophant,
had fawned over.

And to what end? (*Now you hear the mournful picking of a guitar
against the backdrop of the foothills where a cowboy might ride across
the still, undershot Morley sky*)

Twilight brings its chill.
Now comes day's incessant end,
solitary sky,
I watch the red light wane.
The fragrance of the past recedes.

WW2

Good life
Great price

And in September we were at war again
Boys as sweet as ever ready to dash off to their death
And so many girls
Making it their patriotic duty to kiss soldiers good-bye

I'll tell you it affected my bottom line,
All that Vera Lynn and heavy petting
Their innocence took my breath away
Like pain not pleasure

Too Far from the Ground and Not Quite Near Enough to Heaven

What is it about her? She must be getting her bio-text.
What isn't about her? Undoubtedly it's her bio-text.

If it's dog eat dog then she is getting her blood from the bone.
"She's impossible to love" allegedly states her bio-text.

Nature promises to teach us that we have no real virtue,
She is unrepentant, defiantly on her bio-text.

Bleeding heart, bloody heat, bloody sleeve, on the rag, bloody
   gash.
She's bitching once again, repeatedly on her bio-text.

Vagrant whispers inside walls of what went wrong before we
   came.
Who is without sin? she notes angrily in her bio-text.

A woman's work is never done but she's forsaking vengeance.
She's finding a change of heart, earnestly since her bio-text.

She welcomes communion although cliché is still a problem.
Doppleganger found indisputably in her bio-text.

What is it about me? I think I'm getting my bio-text.
What isn't about me? It's absolutely my bio-text.

Stakeout

It was all bound to come to a head. Calgary had gone from frontier town to going concern and a bordello was more past than future. Good wives and sober policemen all harbingers of urban growth.
The edge becoming centre.

Bitterness had me rubbed down. I was tired (once again Calgary was bursting with soldiers) and prideful. Those young men, Constables Ritchie and Timms, had been commanded to take me down a notch. Tasteful decoration and genteel behavior were no longer enough to keep such a public house in business.

It still brings a smile to my face to think of two keen officers, watching my house like boys who found the lady next door naked, hunkered down in the boxcar, being towed into Bowness. I should take pleasure in the lengths they took to bust a madam like me.

Ft. Sask. Prison Blues, 1942
after Ida Cox

That steel door
which is not the polite wood of houses
resonates, stomach drops against the next bad feeling but
pride, still pride sets feet forth

Peeling potatoes becomes metaphor
a walk around the ever shrinking yard
cold cracked hands
the absence here of chatter

Stripped of all that is false
this darkness that cannot be dispensed with
as each day becomes night

Despite its hackneyed sentiment
when given space for consideration
to be found desolate   oh
slow achin' heart disease
consumed by nothing but the blues
being killed by degrees   by
a slow achin' heart   blues ain't
nothin' else but what brought you here

Citrus 1

I was as surprised as anyone. And although I had made a toil of
pleasure, those ladies on American Hill (hearts as hard and small
as nuts), every bit as proud, every bit as haughty, leave me to
ponder about the shape of each fall they took. We have all been
an abomination

By mercy and truth I was purged. Sudden only to those who did
not bear witness, for prison, unlike the army camp, is not filled
with visitors waiting to call on a whore. Still, each day those
soldiers of the Lord made their way to my cell if only to speak
pleasantly of the weather and to leave a copy of the Good Book.
It had been some time since I'd had the leisure to read

Grace came in inches. Not from my jailors who knew little of
common civility but once by the gift of an orange passed to
me with fervent kindness by a clear-eyed girl who remained
unflinching in my presence, and pure. She said, "Better it is to be
of an humble spirit with the lowly, than to divide the spoil with
the proud." I wiped the juice from my chin

And she held my eyes until I smiled at her belief
My knees trembling under the burden of knowing

Revelation

(Having endured the days that brought me to sixty)

A working girl must make a multitude of sacrifices
What is said and what is
Perpetual rhetoric
Where to get what when who and why
Insider/Outsider

Was it so long before the recovery of joy?
Was it fashion?
A lark?
A breakfast of champions?

When planning an exit strategy you should
Consider yourself at home

Don't get me wrong   I was not unhappy

Grace

Let us not look at ourselves differently.
Let us embrace disappointment
Lo, our companion all these many years.
And when we meet our Maker
Let us not forget ourselves
In obsequious acquiescence
In pastoral reflection
Let us embrace the vengeful Creator
Whose wrath and eccentricity
Casts a light upon our own

Let us hold the grudge close to our chests
While we lie in the bed of our own making
Brimming with remorse and resisting
Forgiveness and all it requires of us

Amen

Pearl's Psalter, No. 51

Create in me a clean spirit; wash me and I shall be
whiter than snow
I walk in the balance of God's mercy and judgement
A perfect child, a kitchen, a Sunday dinner
My mother's eyes closed in death, my father's ledgers
A litany of futility
Has left my old aching body
Witness
My sin is ever before me
Cold comfort
A broken and contrite heart
The humility of my sentence

Surprised to be aged and the night still pressing against hope
Good manners could bring me no further

Citrus 2

Before modernity resurrected the Garden of Eden,
before rapid transit,
an orange.
A rarity, however common its skin might feel.

Ladies and Gentlemen:
I have more than one opinion of what you can do with
a drunken sailor.
Shopping will leave you in a constant state of want.

And I pulled the skin back, felt the juice sting
my unkempt fingers,
prepared for the feast of liquid and pulp.
Such a morning to taste an orange!
I turned my back on the simple shy girl.

My body: purity, clarity, insecticide, pesticide, repentance.
Everybody wants what cannot be purchased.

Epiphany

Crying like a baby
Salt in the wound
Hungry as a horse, and
Dropped with a sickening thud

Quiet as a mouse
Bursting at the seams
Trembling with fear
Perched on the wings of a snow-white dove

Reborn

I don't remember my mother
Her straight back and quick laugh
Or she was like my father, dutiful
Strange and cold

Today I am old
Breathless and my blood pounds in my ears
But in the hands of the Shepherd
I am pre-Raphaelite
Unadorned
I have fallen
And I am a child
I am weak
A visible nuisance
A hazard to property value

I am lack of purpose
Forgotten
I am weak
But He is strong

Pearl's Psalter, No. 23

Faith is a painful beauty, skin as clever as a good wife's walls and
her mercy endureth forever.
She preparest me a table of attention, watching, waiting and
always, always ready for a sign.
I'll let you in on a secret; I knew everything before it happened, I
read the Lord like a dime store novel.
I loved the way I love an apocalypse story, with awful dread and
despite myself. I asked and received, asked & asked & asked and
received, presumably no more than I was
capable of.

Forget about the footprints in the sand and all those nights spent
crying at your stupid stupidity. Forget about wanting to stare the
Lord in the eye, to tell Him He expected too much.
And yea, though you've walked through the valley of the shadow
of all that shit, forgive Heaven and whoever else stuck it to you
when you just meant to be a friend.
Finally, it's you who are your Bible, world map and Christ
on the cross.

Surely goodness and mercy shall follow you now that you seek
the still water. Once you were the girl who let the wind lift her
prodigal feet, let it carry you home.
Thank the bruise for the map to your soul it drew upon your
skin. Haven't you been blessed with a profusion of bad feeling,
solid proof that you are exceptional.
You are the shepherd, not much, but enough to get this far and
so you shall not want.

Wide Open Scarlet

I want to tell you girls it will break your heart to leave
crack you open
regardless of relief
same as the moment a girl comprehends
the odds have been unfavourably stacked
against her being anything more

than chattel.   In the houses we clicked our tongues against
the streets, physical safety giving us the illusion
of safety; girls, it's all coming down
you must turn
to a many-roomed mansion and

forgive the cliché. I think it's all right
to let go
regardless of belief
same as leaving the house that reared you
plain and simple really, don't

let anyone tell you otherwise. The civility of
the bordello has been lost to
progress but the Lord
wide open as this prairie sky enjoys
the company of wanton women.

Ministry

Because He is
Perfect past present and future
I went therefore to make disciples of those girls, those
Who heard the echo in their hearts

Because Jesus became sin on my behalf
Whore, cold, rich and lackluster
I retired my jersey so to speak
These are words I love:
Grace
Profligate
Manifest
Illustrious
Edify
Soft
Jubilation

Yes, Thank You Jesus

(Coming up from nothing like you did and
never bucking the will of your Father
Here am I, profligate and resistant
biting the hand that feeds me
But being found and forgiven
I don't want to make less of heaven
Common as a whore, everyday as a wife and
realized on the path of least resistance
These are the days that I had been missing
Now time and meaning converged and
that life was three days ago
I have risen out of the ruin of my living)

You died for a sinner like me

Out of Sight

Just rows and rows of houses
Rock and roll has been born

In my dreams snow is perfect and
My heart is a charmed bean
This little light of mea culpa wrapped
Inside my ribs

I am leaving, ready
For the way on

It all happened to me
I love and don't
Love the obvious

You already know
I'm drawn to magic

Whaiku

Old age brings TV
Miss Kitty, a whore's delight
But more fiction than

Alice just buried
The last of a different age
Another Chinook arches

Girls have cast off boys
They've taken to wearing jeans
A strange enchantment

They think they've started a revolution

Out of Mind

Mom, I say
Tell the girls who Pearl Miller was.
Oh, mom whispers, a sly look on her face
My sisters fidget

Because our mom
Who is surprised to see Mary Jane
Who can't remember what grade my son is in
Or when I work, or that Josette's mother died and
She thinks Sue stole her television remote control and that
Debbie wants her committed.

Our mom who cries if I speak too quickly
And is angry enough to spit,
Is all *50 First Dates* but not so pretty.

Oh, mom whispers, suddenly a clever little girl,
She was a famous whore, you know.

Photo by Deborah Cullen

Nancy Jo Cullen lives in Calgary with her kids,
cat, and gecko. Her first collection of poetry,
Science Fiction Saint, was short-listed for the Gerald
Lampert Award for best first book of poetry, the
Writers Guild of Alberta's Stephan G. Stephansson
award for poetry and the Book Publishers
Association of Alberta's best trade book.